Dear Parent:
Your child's love of reading starts here!

Every child learns to read in a different way and at his or her own speed. Some go back and forth between reading levels and read favorite books again and again. Others read through each level in order. You can help your young reader improve and become more confident by encouraging his or her own interests and abilities. From books your child reads with you to the first books he or she reads alone, there are I Can Read Books for every stage of reading:

SHARED READING
Basic language, word repetition, and whimsical illustrations, ideal for sharing with your emergent reader

BEGINNING READING
Short sentences, familiar words, and simple concepts for children eager to read on their own

READING WITH HELP
Engaging stories, longer sentences, and language play for developing readers

READING ALONE
Complex plots, challenging vocabulary, and high-interest topics for the independent reader

ADVANCED READING
Short paragraphs, chapters, and exciting themes for the perfect bridge to chapter books

I Can Read Books have introduced children to the joy of reading since 1957. Featuring award-winning authors and illustrators and a fabulous cast of beloved characters, I Can Read Books set the standard for beginning readers.

A lifetime of discovery begins with the magical words **"I Can Read!"**

Visit www.icanread.com for information
on enriching your child's reading experience.

To Daisy

I Can Read Book® is a trademark of HarperCollins Publishers.
Balzer + Bray is an imprint of HarperCollins Publishers.

Otter: The Best Job Ever!

ISBN 978-0-06-236654-2 (pbk. bdg.) — ISBN 978-0-06-236655-9 (trade bdg.)

16 17 18   PC/WOR   10 9 8 7 6 5 4 3 2

❖

First Edition

OTTER
The Best Job Ever!

By SAM GARTON

BALZER + BRAY

An Imprint of HarperCollins*Publishers*

Otter Keeper has a job.

Teddy and I do not have jobs.

This is not fair at all.

We want to have jobs too.

"What jobs can we do?"
I ask Teddy.

Teddy says he wants
to be an acrobat.

I help him jump very high.

Oh no!

Teddy is not good at landing.

I have to dry him off.
Acrobat is not the right job
for Teddy.

Teddy says he wants to be
an explorer.

I help him explore lots of
fun places.

Oh no!

Teddy gets stuck.

I have to save him. Explorer

is not the right job for Teddy.

Now Teddy wants to be
a cook.

I show him how to make
yummy foods.

Oh no!

Teddy makes a big mess.

I help him clean up.
Cook is not the right job
for Teddy.

Teddy is sad.

He has run out of jobs.

"You do not need a job,
Teddy," I say.

"You can be my best friend."

Teddy is very good at being
my best friend.

Oh no!

I forgot to find a job for me.

I tell Otter Keeper
my problem.

He gives me a hug.

I feel a lot better.

"You already have a big job," says Otter Keeper.

My job is to take care of
Teddy.

I am very good at my job.